THINGS
WITH
WINGS

Ostriches
Nature's Biggest Birds

Frankie Stout

PowerKiDS
press.
New York

To my dad

Published in 2009 by The Rosen Publishing Group, Inc.
29 East 21st Street, New York, NY 10010

First Edition

Editor: Nicole Pristash
Book Design: Kate Laczynski
Photo Researcher: Jessica Gerweck

Photo Credits: Cover, p. 1 © www.istockphoto.com/L. Timothy Terry; pp. 5, 7, 19, 21 Shutterstock.com; p. 7 (inset) © www.istockphoto.com/Stephanie Phillips; p. 9 © BIOS Denis-Huot M. & C./Peter Arnold, Inc.; p. 11 © Andoni Canela/Age Fotostock; p. 13 © www.istockphoto.com/Roman Kazmin; p. 15 © Gallo Images-Martin Harvey/Getty Images; p. 17 © Harvey Martin/Bios/Peter Arnold, Inc.

Library of Congress Cataloging-in-Publication Data

Stout, Frankie.
  Ostriches : nature's biggest birds / Frankie Stout. — 1st ed.
      p. cm. — (Things with wings)
  Includes index.
  ISBN 978-1-4042-4498-6 (library binding)
  1. Ostriches—Juvenile literature. I. Title.
  QL696.S9S78 2009
  598.5'24—dc22
                                                    2008007514

Oct'08

Manufactured in the United States of America

CONTENTS

What Is an Ostrich?

Do you know what an ostrich is? The ostrich is the largest type of bird on Earth. People sometimes call ostriches camel birds because their large size, long necks, and long legs make them look like camels.

Ostriches have feathers and wings on their bodies, but they cannot fly. They are too large to fly. **Female** ostriches have brown feathers on their wings, and **male** ostriches have black and white feathers.

Do you want to know more? Let's learn some more fun things about ostriches, like where they live, what they eat, and how fast they run!

Ostriches can live for quite a long time. They generally live for 30 to 70 years.

Strange Birds

Ostriches do not look like other birds. Most birds are small, but ostriches can be up to 9 feet (3 m) tall. Some weigh up to 340 pounds (154 kg). These birds are larger than an adult person!

Ostriches have round, heavy bodies covered in feathers, but their long legs and long necks are **bare**. Ostriches have small heads with big, strong bills. Their strong feet have two toes. One of these toes has a large nail that forms a claw. Ostriches' feet are great for running fast. They can run up to 40 miles per hour (64 km/h)!

An ostrich's eyes are almost 2 inches (5 cm) wide. *Inset:* An ostrich can use the sharp claw on each of its feet to hit an animal that is trying to hurt the ostrich.

What Are Their Wings For?

Ostriches have wings, but they cannot fly. Instead, ostriches use their wings in other ways. By opening and moving its wings as it runs, an ostrich can **steer** its body where it wants to go. It uses its wings to steer its body the way a driver uses a steering wheel to steer a fast car. An ostrich's wings also keep its body **balanced** when it runs.

Ostriches also use their wings to find **mates**. Male ostriches open and shake their wings to get female ostriches to notice them. Even though ostriches cannot fly, their wings do many important jobs!

Here an ostrich is shown spreading its wings open while it runs. Doing this will help the ostrich stay balanced so it can run for a long time.

Where Do Ostriches Live?

Ostriches live in the savannas and the deserts of Africa. A savanna is a place where there is a lot of grass, along with some trees. A savanna is semiarid, which means it is dry for much of the year. Deserts are sandy and dry. Both places get very little rain.

Ostriches can live in these dry places because they can go without water for a long time. They live off the water that is found on the plants they eat. Ostriches do like water when they can find it, though. They love to take baths in the watering holes they find.

This ostrich is taking a drink from a watering hole in Africa. Ostriches are used to going a long time without water, but they still take a drink when they can.

Birds in Herds

Most ostriches live in small groups, called herds. These herds are made up of around 10 ostriches. However, some herds have had up to 100 ostriches in them. In a group, if an ostrich sees a **predator** coming, it can let the other birds know. Ostriches can see danger coming from far away because they have very good eyesight. Being in a herd helps ostriches stay safe from their predators.

Ostrich herds sometimes group together with zebras or antelopes. These animals like to eat from the same grasslands of the savanna, and ostriches live peacefully with them.

Here you can see two ostriches and a zebra herd. These two kinds of animals have learned to live together in deserts and grasslands without hurting each other.

Picky Eaters

Ostriches eat seeds, leaves, and even lizards and bugs. They pick at the ground and at plants, eating what they can find. Like all birds, ostriches do not have teeth. Instead, an ostrich swallows sand and small stones to help it eat. The stones and sand **grind** the food before the ostrich swallows it. The stones do not hurt them, though. Ostriches have strong stomachs, called gizzards, which can hold the stones and sand.

As they eat, ostriches raise their heads a lot. This is so they can see if predators are around. Ostriches are always on the lookout!

Plants and bugs can be hard to eat, so an ostrich eats small stones to help grind up its food. An ostrich generally carries around 2 pounds (1 kg) of stones in its stomach!

15

Ostrich Predators

Ostriches and ostrich chicks have to watch out for predators, such as lions, cheetahs, **hyenas**, and **vultures**. An ostrich will try to scare smaller predators away by opening its wings and shaking its feathers. If a larger animal is coming, an ostrich will run away. If it cannot run away, it will kick the predator.

Another thing ostriches do when they are in danger is lie down on the ground. This way, the ostrich looks like a mound of earth. From far away, predators cannot tell where the ostrich is. An ostrich has to be smart to keep itself and its babies safe.

These hyenas are about to eat some ostrich eggs. Hyenas are some of the most dangerous ostrich predators.

Eggs and Baby Chicks

Ostriches have their babies in the dry season. First, the lead male ostrich in a herd will make a nest in the dirt. The lead female ostrich in the herd will lay her eggs first. Then other females in the herd also lay their eggs in the nest.

The lead male and the lead female take turns keeping all the eggs warm. After about six weeks, the chicks **hatch**. The new chicks have soft feathers and are a light brown color. Soon after they hatch, the chicks are able to run and follow their mothers and fathers around.

When an ostrich chick is born, it is only 10 inches (25 cm) tall. The chick then grows 10 to 12 inches (25–30 cm) every month in its first year!

19

Ostrich Farms

One thing you may not know about ostriches is that people all over the world farm them. Farming means raising ostriches and keeping them on farms. Ostriches are farmed mostly for their feathers, which are made into dusters that are used for cleaning.

Some people hunt ostriches. These people use ostrich skin to make bags or shoes. Some people eat ostrich meat as well. If too many ostriches are hunted, they can die out. For now, there are many ostriches left in the world. At one time, though, ostriches were hunted and became **extinct** in parts of Asia.

This ostrich is sitting inside its pen at an ostrich farm. Ostriches are farmed in more than 50 countries around the world.

Ostriches on Earth

Ostriches are an interesting part of our Earth. Like all animals, they are important to our **planet**. They are a lasting part of our Earth that should be kept safe from people who want to hurt them.

You will not find ostriches in your backyard. If you ever visit Africa, you might get to see ostriches in a group with antelopes and zebras. You might also be able to see an ostrich at the zoo. If you do see one, you will know that you are looking at one of nature's most special birds!

GLOSSARY

balanced (BAL-ensd) Staying steady.

bare (BER) Not covered.

extinct (ek-STINKT) No longer around.

female (FEE-mayl) Having to do with women and girls.

grind (GRYND) To break into small pieces.

hatch (HACH) To come out of an egg.

hyenas (hy-EE-nuhz) Wolflike animals that eat other animals.

male (MAYL) Having to do with men and boys.

mates (MAYTS) Pairs for making babies.

planet (PLA-net) A large object, such as Earth, that moves around the Sun.

predator (PREH-duh-ter) An animal that kills other animals for food.

steer (STEER) To make something go in a certain direction.

vultures (VUL-churz) Large birds that feed on the dead meat of other animals.

INDEX

B
bills, 6, 14
bird(s), 4, 6, 12, 22
body, 4, 6, 8

C
camels, 4
chicks, 16, 18

E
Earth, 4, 22

F
feathers, 4, 6, 16, 20
feet, 6

H
heads, 6, 14
hyenas, 16

L
legs, 4, 6

N
necks, 4, 6

P
predator(s), 12, 14, 1

S
stones, 14

V
vultures, 16

WEB SITES

Due to the changing nature of Internet links, PowerKids Press has developed an online list of Web sites related to the subject of this book. This site is updated regularly. Please use this link to access the list:
www.powerkidslinks.com/wings/ostrich/